YOUR KNOWLEDGE HAS VALUE

AF141604

- We will publish your bachelor's and master's thesis, essays and papers

- Your own eBook and book - sold worldwide in all relevant shops

- Earn money with each sale

Upload your text at www.GRIN.com and publish for free

Kevin Rudolph

Aus der Reihe: e-fellows.net stipendiaten-wissen

e-fellows.net (Hrsg.)

Band 1214

The Use of Ontologies in Practice

GRIN Publishing

Bibliographic information published by the German National Library:

The German National Library lists this publication in the National Bibliography; detailed bibliographic data are available on the Internet at http://dnb.dnb.de .

This book is copyright material and must not be copied, reproduced, transferred, distributed, leased, licensed or publicly performed or used in any way except as specifically permitted in writing by the publishers, as allowed under the terms and conditions under which it was purchased or as strictly permitted by applicable copyright law. Any unauthorized distribution or use of this text may be a direct infringement of the author s and publisher s rights and those responsible may be liable in law accordingly.

Imprint:

Copyright © 2015 GRIN Verlag GmbH
Print and binding: Books on Demand GmbH, Norderstedt Germany
ISBN: 978-3-656-97611-0

This book at GRIN:

http://www.grin.com/en/e-book/300018/the-use-of-ontologies-in-practice

GRIN - Your knowledge has value

Since its foundation in 1998, GRIN has specialized in publishing academic texts by students, college teachers and other academics as e-book and printed book. The website www.grin.com is an ideal platform for presenting term papers, final papers, scientific essays, dissertations and specialist books.

Visit us on the internet:

http://www.grin.com/

http://www.facebook.com/grincom

http://www.twitter.com/grin_com

ONTOLOGIES IN PRACTICE

Seminar Report

Student: Kevin Rudolph

Abstract:

Most of today's information systems are highly heterogeneous and complex. High efforts and costs are put into interlinking systems to let systems communicate to each other and thus overcoming heterogeneity. The semantic web plays a significant role in the way it covers and links knowledge, making the web's content understandable for machine-to-machine interactions. Hereby, ontologies serve as a technology to cover, infer and verify knowledge and making it available to accomplish a common understanding among participating agents.

This paper describes how ontologies are used in practice to support the overcoming of heterogeneity in information systems. After a revision of basic semantic technologies and standards like OWL and SPARQL we discuss a variety of methods and tools of the semantic web. In more detail, we investigate ontology editors, especially the Protégé tool as a well-established open-source application to create, edit and share ontologies. At last, we discover a variety of practical applications where ontologies are of high use.

Keywords: Ontology Editors
Protégé
Semantic Web Technologies
Heterogeneity
Information Integration

20.01.2014
WINTER TERM 2014/15
"AIM1 - HETEROGENEOUS DISTRIBUTED INFORMATION SYSTEMS"
Database Systems and Information Management
Berlin Institute of Technology

Content

1. Introduction 3

2. Revision of Semantic Concepts 3

   2.1 Knowledge and Semantic Web 3

      2.1.1 DIKW Pyramid 3

      2.1.3 Description Logics 5

   2.2 Ontologies, XML and RDF(S) 5

      2.2.1 Ontologies 5

      2.2.2 XML 6

      2.2.3 RDF(S) 6

   2.3 OWL and SPARQL 7

      2.3.1 OWL 7

      2.3.2 SPARQL 7

3. Ontology-based Information Integration 7

   3.1 Methods 7

      3.1.1 Mappings 8

      3.1.2 Ontology Integration Architectures 8

      3.1.3 Reasoning, Inferring, Expert Systems 9

   3.2 Tools 10

      3.2.1 Semantic Web Tools 10

      3.2.2 Ontology Editors 10

4. Ontology Editor - Protégé 11

   4.1 General Background 12

   4.2 Historical Background 12

   4.3 Features 14

   4.4 Internals 15

   4.5 Building Ontologies 17

   4.6 Critical Appraisal 17

5. Practical Applications 17

   5.1 Industry Solutions 17

   5.2 Established Ontologies 18

   5.3 Biomedical Science and Protégé 18

6. Conclusion 19

7. References 20

1. Introduction

Enormous costs and efforts arise when it comes to information and data integration of distributed and heterogeneous information systems with the intention to create value. Often it is a challenge to establish a base for a common agreed understanding of the content of knowledge bases. For example, in the field of medicine a tremendous amount of expert terms builds the knowledge physicians have to work with. Those terms are related and have logic interrelations to other terms.

The web has a high potential as a platform to store and share knowledge. The problem is that web content was initially made to be understandable for human users, not machines. Thus, the meaning of terms and phrases is not necessarily clear to non-human agents. In addition, defective system can be the result.

The semantic web plays a role as a web concept where the semantic meaning of the web content is clarified and can be examined and analyzed. A very valuable ability is to infer new knowledge. Ontologies can help in this case as they are formal and explicit representations of concepts with intrinsic logical relationships. The W3C and the open-source community developed a variety of standards to represent ontologies in an expressive, formal and explicit way - also containing semantic relationships. Furthermore, a lot of methods and tools are available to support programmers, scientists and decision makers in the creation of ontologies. Especially, the ontology editor Protégé is a well-established tool to create, edit, visualize and to reason ontologies.

The remainder of this paper is organized as follows: Section 2 revises some of the fundamental semantic concepts necessary to create ontologies in OWL - The Web Ontology Language. Section 3 is devoted to a description of methods and tools for information integration based on ontologies. In section 4 we present the Protégé tool and discuss it's characteristics in detail. Section 5 gives insight in some major practical applications where ontologies are used. Section 6 concludes the main findings.

2. Revision of Semantic Concepts

Semantic concepts are technologies and standards to describe the content of the web in a machine-readable format enriched by semantic meanings and logical interrelations between terms. In this section we give insight in the definition of knowledge and the interdependencies between semantic web technologies. Furthermore, we define the basics of logics. They are represented in ontologies to infer new knowledge from existing domain concepts. Various technologies are used to build up OWL (Web Ontology Language) and SPARQL (SPARQL Protocol And RDF Query Language) to represent and query knowledge in ontologies.

2.1 Knowledge and Semantic Web
2.1.1 DIKW Pyramid

For the understanding of the semantic web it is necessary to understand what knowledge is about. Regarding to the knowledge pyramid information is raw data extended by meaning, whereas knowledge is information extended by a context. Thus, it is obvious that knowledge can be implied by some information base and a context. Later we will call this approach reasoning (see Chapter 3.1). Figure 1 illustrates an adapted version of the original knowledge pyramid extended by examples [9],[36].

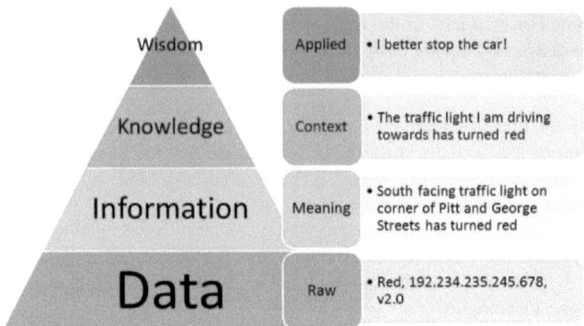

Figure 1 - DIKW (Data Information Knowledge Wisdom) Pyramid [9]

2.1.2 Semantic Web Technology Stack

The semantic web technology stack (Figure 2) comprises the standards and technologies of the semantic web. According to this the foundation layer of the stack encompasses the standards for symbols and resources as a web platform. URIs (Unique Resource Identifiers) as an identification technology for web content serves using a web protocol like HTTP (Hypertext Transfer Protocol). Sharing of structured information is supported by solutions like XML (Extensible Markup Language). The creation of graph-based data models is done for example with the RDF model (Resource Description Framework) incorporating the URIs. Supported by a strong vocabulary and logical interdependencies OWL (Web Ontology Language) can then serve as the global language of ontologies, with even more expressiveness than RDFS (RDF Schema). On the top logical interdependencies built into the proofing module and OWL guarantees the ability to infer knowledge and the gathering of new relations [36].

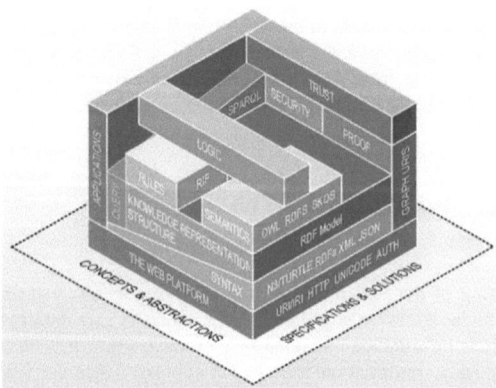

Figure 2 - Semantic Web Technology Stack [28]

2.1.3 Description Logics

Unlike propositional logic which only deals with entire propositions and first order logic which has an inefficient problem solving capability, description logic is expressive enough to represent information with their semantics and offering the logical capability to infer new knowledge [4]. Furthermore, properties are very formal. Reasoning algorithms are well-known. Basic logics in description logics include:

- Atomic negations
- Concept intersection
- Universal restrictions
- Limited existing quantification
- Nominal
- Inverse properties
- Cardinality restrictions

2.2 Ontologies, XML and RDF(S)

To understand the later OWL technology it is essential to carefully investigate the properties of ontologies. OWL is constructed by the synthesis of several basic technologies like XML and RDF(S).

2.2.1 Ontologies

As Gruber formulated, an ontology is "an explicit, formal specification of a shared conceptualization" [17]. Thus, it represents concepts and their relationships within a specific domain in a formal and explicit way. As we have already seen ontologies can be modelled and analyzed with technologies of the semantic web technology stack.

Ontologies have several purposes. They are needed to represent a shared common knowledge of a specific domain and facilitate the reuse and analysis of this knowledge. Furthermore, they declare semantics explicitly and enable the knowledge sharing among various agents like software or people. Also, ontologies are helpful to make clear expressive statements.

An ontology consists of classes and their properties, as well as individuals (instances) and semantic relationships [31],[44]. Some of the most used relationships are:
- Meronymy ("part of")
- Holonymy ("the whole of")
- Synonymy ("equal")
- Antonomy ("opposite")
- Hyponymy (specialization)
- Hypernymy (generalization)

Figure 3 shows an example of an ontology about pizzas. As we can see the ontology helps to clarify what a "cheesy pizza" is. We can identify specializations like "CheesyPizza is a Pizza" as well as special relations like "CheesyPizza hasTopping CheeseTopping".

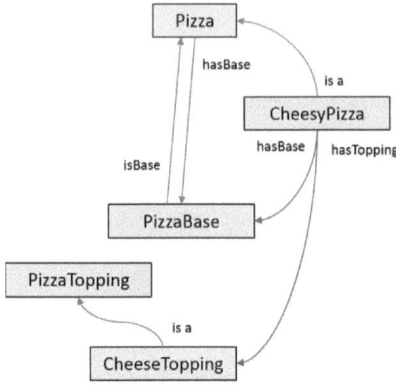

Figure 3 - Exemplary pizza ontology (based on [20])

2.2.2 XML

XML (Extensible Markup Language) is a tag-based meta-language. All elements, attributes and content is defined by named markup tags. The content is always plain string text or other tags with content arranged in a tree structure.

From this point of view XML is marginally useful to build knowledge in some extent since it provides a sharable format, is a widely spread web standard and able to develop markup languages for domains. Ultimately, XML can only describe syntax but no semantics and relations. XML tags are rather meaningless for software agents [31].

2.2.3 RDF(S)

RDF (Resource Description Framework) is a data model to provide the internet with metadata. Its core are triple statements to describe resources and attributes in a simple subject-predicate-object relation whereas the subject is the resource, the predicate the relation and the object a resource or literal.

On the one hand RDF supports formalizing knowledge in the way it describes semantics in a machine-readable, formal, explicit and standardized way. One the other hand it neither offers a format to convey content nor it can describe knowledge on an instance level. There is still a lack in complexity to describe ontologies with RDF. A combination of RDF/XML would lead to a possibility to represent the syntax too. However, it would not be possible to represent class descriptions.

RDFS (RDF Schema) compensates some of the disadvantages RDF struggles with to represent ontologies. It is a domain-neutral, formal schema language which provides a basis structure for classes and their properties. At this point we still miss some features to represent ontologies e.g. advanced logics to infer new knowledge out of existing knowledge [31].

2.3 OWL and SPARQL

The two most widespread standards in the area of the creation of ontologies are OWL and SPARQL. Ontology editors make highly use of them. Other ontology standards are SHOE and OIL (DAML+OIL).

2.3.1 OWL

OWL stands for "Web Ontology Language" and is a W3C standard. It extends the former semantic standards by expressive definitions of classes and properties, as well as semantics based on description logic. There are two OWL versions (OWL 1.0, 2004 and OWL 2.0, 2009) and three sub-languages (OWL Lite, OWL DL and OWL Full) available. The sub-languages differ in that extent that they contain a distinct expressiveness and decidability. OWL is known as the de-facto language of global ontologies. Based on a strong vocabulary and expressive description logic utilization consistency and satisfiability of ontologies can be checked. Furthermore, reasoning and inference of new knowledge is supported [21],[37].

OWL elements include namespaces, an ontology header (with metadata about the ontology), class and subclass definitions, properties and their characteristics, restrictions, maps and individuals. The new vocabulary includes many options to logically combine classes (disjunction, equivalence, complement), restrict relations by cardinalities and define properties of properties through transitivity, symmetry, functional and inverse.

2.3.2 SPARQL

SPARQL is a graph-based RDF query language to query RDF and OWL documents. Query triples do match data triples. As a result of a query a combination of matches will be delivered. The syntax is similar to SQL (SELECT, FROM, WHERE clauses). A SPARQL query consists of a prefix (namespace URIs), a query results clause (results forms, dataset sources and query pattern) and optional query modifiers [41].

3. Ontology-based Information Integration

A variety of methods and tools exist to overcome heterogeneity in information systems with the help of ontologies and the semantic web. Ontologies support the process in a way that they enable the automatic and semantic-oriented interoperability between machines. Supporting methods and concepts are mainly mappings, architectural styles and reasoners. Many tools like semantic frameworks or ontology editors are available to programmers and engineers to convey their concepts into practice [36].

3.1 Methods

Semantic heterogeneity is defined by a diverging semantic interpretation of the meaning that can be concluded when investigating a schema. With the help of ontologies and their logical interdependencies concepts can be inferred by implicit semantics in the schema. With the specification and the shared knowledge of a domain followed by logical inference semantic heterogeneity can be overcome.

Ontologies help to link semantically heterogenic systems as it delivers a vocabulary to describe concepts and relations of formal models. Furthermore, they act as global schemas of the mediation layer, a layer of indirection between users/applications and the data source layer. They offer explicit definitions of terms and relationships to be interpreted accurately from multiple different sources. In addition, ontologies provide a global query schema and verification techniques to guarantee the correctness between multiple sources [1],[36].

3.1.1 Mappings

A mapping is an essential method to transform various schemas into an integrated data schema. Two different map concepts are used, the Global-as-View (GAV) and the Local-as-View (LAV). The GAV describes that every entity in the global schema is mapped to the data sources. Whereby, the LAV method means that every entity in the sources is mapped to the global schema. Furthermore, there exist approaches to map ontologies to information sources or even ontologies to other ontologies [13],[45],[46],[50]. Figure 4 shows the conceptually role of a mapper as a tool for semantic data integration. Hereby, ontologies, thesauri (controlled and interconnected vocabulary) and other sources are mapped to build semantically integrated data. In [8] are number of ontology mapping tools as well as advantages and drawbacks of mappings are discussed.

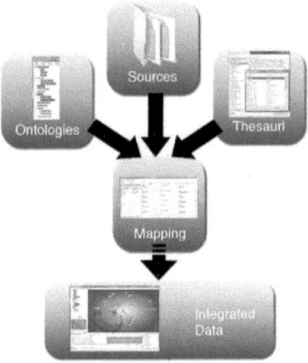

Figure 4 - The role of mappings in the workflow
of semantic integration [45]

3.1.2 Ontology Integration Architectures

There exist different approaches to design an architecture for ontology-based integration systems (Figure 5). The very simple single ontology approach illustrates that a single global ontology is accessed by various different agents. In this method no integration is used. In the multiple ontology approach each local ontology is an individual data source and connected to other ontologies. Complex mappings are used to create this flexible architecture.
The hybrid ontology approach links the former both methodologies to that extent that a shared global ontology is build out of a number of local ontologies. Although this is a complicated approach it makes it simple to integrate and reuse several knowledge domains [50].

3.1.3 Reasoning, Inferring, Expert Systems

Semantic reasoning is a valuable feature applied on ontologies to check semantic relationships and infer new insights of (integrated) ontologies. Semantic reasoners are software concepts and solutions that conclude logical consequences from a set of axioms and facts. Ontology languages like OWL and description languages are used. Semantic reasoning can be done for example by inference engines, probabilistic reasoning, fuzzy reasoning, etc. An inference engine typically deduces the new knowledge by applying logical if-then rules. Originally, inference engines were used in expert systems, computer systems that emulate the decision making ability of human experts in a certain field [50].

Single ontology approach

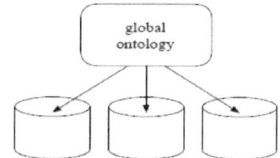

Multiple ontology approach

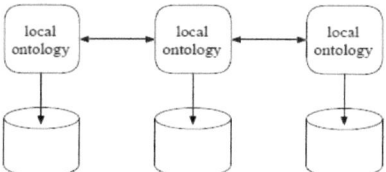

Hybrid ontology approach

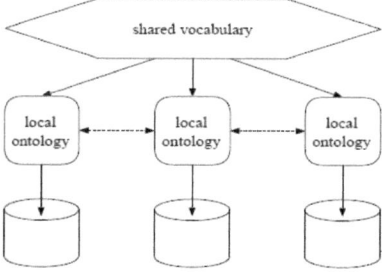

Figure 5 - Ontology integration architectures [50]

3.2 Tools

3.2.1 Semantic Web Tools

There is a huge variety of tools available to develop semantic web components and systems dealing with semantic concepts. Semantic web tools can be divided into several tool classes. Ontology editors help to create, edit and visualize ontologies. Inference machines and reasoners are able to conclude new knowledge and validate existing ontologies. RDF-izers are capable to transform non-RDF data like plain text into RDF format data, which then can be stored in triplestores, a specialized database for triples. Semantic web development toolkits are very useful multi-use tools to develop comprehensive semantic web solutions. They integrate several other techniques. Semantic web browsers use URIs to retrieve data from the web and make it available to the user. Semantic knowledge bases are large stores of data extracted from various sources to offer an integrated knowledge base of a certain domain [27]. In Table 1 we created an overview of the most important semantic web tool classes, with their corresponding purposes and a list of well-established tools.

Tool class	Purpose	Example
Ontology Editor	Edit and visualize ontologies	Protégé, TopBraid, Altova, Swoop
Inference Machines/Reasoners	Concluding knowledge; Validating	Pallet, KAON2, FACT++, Racer, HermiT
RDF-izer	Transform non-RDF data into RDF	Triplify, D2RQ platform,
Triplestore	Database for triples (RDF)	3Store, AllegroGraph, 4Store
Semantic Web Development Toolkit	Multi-use development framework	Jena, CubicWeb, Sesame, JRDF
Semantic Web Browser	Using URIs directly to retrieve data from the web	Snorql, EulerGUI, LinkSailor, mSpace, BrowseRDF
Semantic Knowledge Base	Large store of data extracted from various sources	WordNet, ConceptNet, SemNet

Table 1 - Semantic web tools: classes, purposes and examples (based on [27])

3.2.2 Ontology Editors

Ontology editors are applications to create, edit, visualize and integrate ontologies in various formats. Figure 6 illustrates some of the most important features. Features of ontology editors can be categorized into three classes: user-oriented, internal and external features. User-oriented features are those which are directly connected to the editing user. Thus, a user should be capable with an appropriate ontology editor to design ontologies with the help of graphical interfaces, to visualize the ontology (e.g. in a 2D-Graph) and to be supported in the development by guidelines. Internal features include those which characterize the internal architecture. Usually, ontology editors are capable to import and export ontologies, and also to integrate ontology reasoners and inference engines. From an external point of view ontology editors should be capable to collaborate with other development tools, data formats and languages.

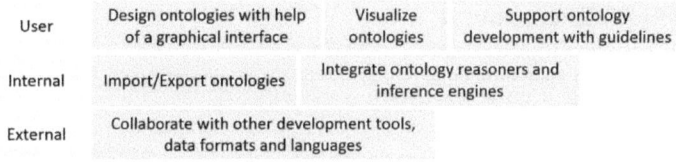

Figure 6 - Features of ontology editors (own illustration)

A currently modern trend is the ability of ontology editors to support collaborative work on ontologies. Those tools and tool extensions need the same level of expressiveness as standalone editors extended by some collaborative-enabling features [18] like:

- User management
- History tracking
- Version management
- Synchronous/asynchronous editing
- Discussions and annotations

In Table 2 we display some of the most used ontology editors in practice. Most of the tools are multipurpose ontology editors, like Protégé and the NeOn Toolkit. Some others have specific purposes. For example, Anzo Express is a tool to build ontologies based on Microsoft Excel sheets which makes it a nice tool to easily create ontologies ad-hoc out of standard office applications and formats. The Fluent Editor is an ontology editor to use natural language as a knowledge modeling language. A more detailed comparison of various ontology editors can be found in [3].

Ontology Editor	Differentiation remarks
Protégé	Multipurpose
NeOn Toolkit	Multipurpose
SWOOP	Multipurpose
TopBraid Composer	Multipurpose
Vitro	Multipurpose
Anzo Express	Microsoft Excel integration
OWLGrEd	Focus on visualization
Fluent Editor	Natural language representation

Table 2 - Ontology editors and their differentiation remarks (own illustration)

4. Ontology Editor - Protégé

As a specific semantic web tool we choose Protégé. It is an ontology editor highly used in practical surroundings by science and practical applications (e.g. in the biomedical science [5]). After a description of some general background of Progégé we will discover the main stages of its 26 years of history. It follows a detailed look onto some of the main features and internal architectures. In the last section we describe how to build ontologies with Protégé and discuss Protégé in a critical field.

4.1 General Background

Protégé is an open source ontology editor developed by the Stanford Medical Informatics group. On its website [23] it is described as the following: "Protégé is a free, open-source platform that provides a growing user community with a suite of tools to construct domain models and knowledge-based applications with ontologies." Originally, Protégé was developed to create knowledge databases for medical research. It is written in Java. Many plugins are available (e.g. visualization, inference, import/export) to expand the tool's capabilities. A Java API is available for developers. As an ontology editor Protégé concentrates on the editing, validation and visualization of ontologies. Moreover, it is a development environment with many connectors e.g. to the Jena framework. Protégé supports OWL DL and some parts of OWL Full.

Originally, there are two ways to model knowledge in Protégé: with Protégé-frames and Protégé-OWL. Protégé-frames are hierarchical structures of concepts, slots and attributes whereas Protégé-OWL is conceptually based on OWL and thus includes description logics for inference mechanisms and to imply knowledge. Some concepts are necessary to understand how Protégé-frames and Protégé-OWL handle semantics differently: The unique name assumption and the closed world assumption fulfilled only by Protégé-frames and the open world assumption fulfilled by Protégé-OWL. The unique name assumption assumes that different names necessarily correspond to different things unless stated otherwise. On the other hand the closed world assumption refers to the fact that a statement is always wrong when it does not exist in the knowledge base. This proves the fact that Protégé-frames are not capable to infer interrelationships between terms in the knowledge base, whereas Protégé-OWL is always able to infer e.g. equivalent objects by itself. For Protégé-OWL the open world assumption means that everything can be integrated unless no constraints are violated [52].

Through its history of 26 years where Protégé-I was released in 1988, the newest version today is also available as a web-based ontology editor for collaborative editing called WebProtégé. There is still a standalone version offered called Protégé Desktop in its version 5.0 beta [15],[23].

4.2 Historical Background

The evolution of Protégé (Figure 7) originates from a tool with a single specific purpose which is very different from the manifold purposes it fits today. The first tool released was named Protégé-I (1988). It was meant to be a tool used by knowledge engineers to design knowledge-acquisition tools which than could be used by domain experts to create knowledge bases. Protégé-I could not handle any semantics. It's only purpose laid in the field of medicine.

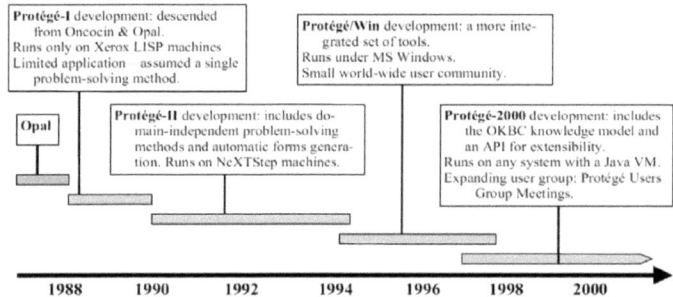

Figure 7 - History of Protégé (1988-2010) [15]

Two years after the release of Protégé-I, Protégé-II (1990) was released. Protégé-II was able to use multi-purpose ontologies and also to map ontologies between knowledge bases. Whereas Protégé-I and Protégé-II run on Xerox LISP and NeXTStep machines, respectively, Protégé/Win (1994) was available under MS Windows. Moreover, Protégé/Win was meant to be an ontology editor by the definition we present in chapter 3.2.2. With the release of Protégé-2000 (1997) a widely accepted, scalable, flexible and extensible ontology editor was available, also capable to edit large knowledge bases. Furthermore, it was capable to support RDF formats and connections to other databases.

Today Protégé Desktop (on the basis of Protégé-2000) and WebProtégé are the newest releases of the Protégé-tool. Recent achieved milestones for Protégé Desktop include its capability to handle OWL 2.0 formats, to offer in-memory connections to reasoners for enhanced performance and even more plug-ins and extensions. It is also capable to to serve with collaborative functions (Collaborative Protégé). Furthermore, a lot of modules are optimized like reasoning support, GUI framework, modularization and navigation. WebProtégé serves as a fully web-based ontology editor capable to offer many collaboration features like change tracking, revision history, user access management, notes, discussion, notifications [24]. In Figure 8 we present a screenshot of Desktop-Protégé in its newest version Protégé 5.0 beta. For comparison, Figure 9 illustrates the graphical user interface of WebProtégé.

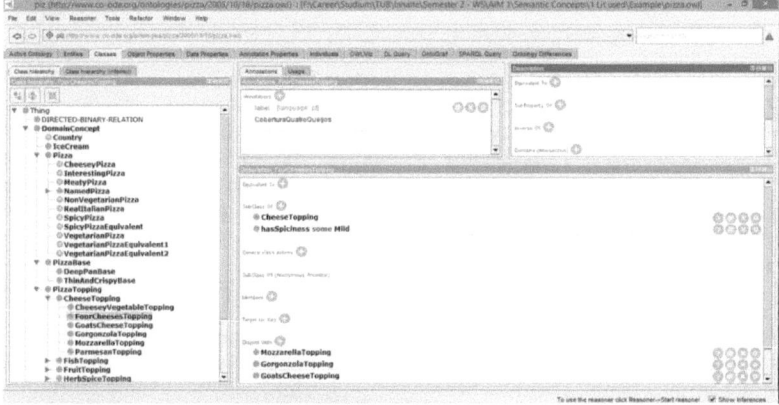

Figure 8 - Screenshot of Protégé 5.0 beta with open "Classes"-tab

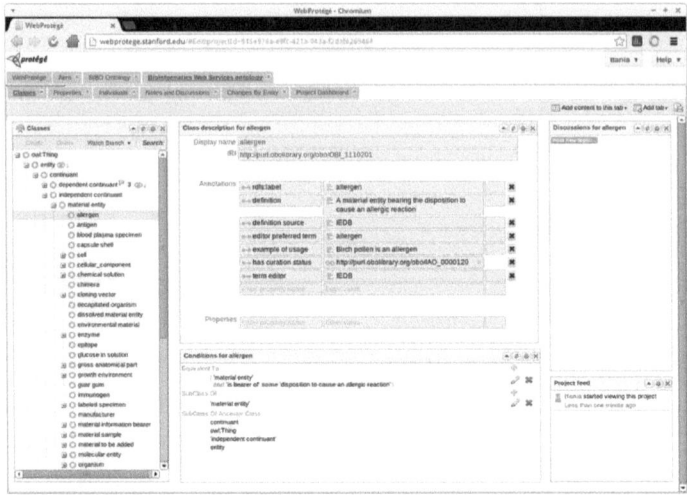

Figure 9 - Screenshot of WebProtégé with open "Classes"-tab [24]

4.3 Features

Many features for Protégé are available as plugins in a plugin library. The main groups are natural language processing, biomedical informatics, export/import, querying, reasoning, validation and visualization. Plugins can serve in many ways, e.g. as a tab widget, slot widget, backend, project or export plugin.

One of the most interesting features of Protégé is its capability to process natural language. Usual text can semi-automatically be transformed into ontologies. Users still have to intervene in some cases with acceptations and rejections of proposals. Thus, validity and integrity is increased. A well-established plugin for this purpose is the DOG4DAG generator. The generator is capable to define terms and definitions as well as to create semantic relationships between terms. Ontologies are automatically mapped to other ontologies for more data retrieval [51].

Another important feature is semantic reasoning. Semantic reasoning is available with Protégé 4 in its standard version and through third-party plugins. Reasoners differ a lot based on expressivity, practical usability and performance. One common-used example is RacerProTG. Core element is a description logic reasoner. Tasks fulfilled by RacerProTG are: consistency checks, concept satisfiability checks, implicit subclass relationship deduction, synonym finding, prediction of computational query effort and covering axiom revolving [19],[42]. A very comprehensive comparison of various reasoners can be found in [10].

A large variety of visualization techniques and tools facilitate simple communication of ontologies to human users. A simple standard way is the indented list in form of a hierarchy, often found in the class browser. A more vivid approach delivers a node-link/tree visualization. This method is widely used (e.g. by OntoViz and OntoGraf). More advanced approaches are three dimensional visualization techniques, for example as a three-dimensional directed graph or 3D-information landscapes. Visualization techniques for ontologies are particularly used in practice [2],[32].

Two visualization tools are widely used in Protégé: OntoViz [26] and OntoGraf [25]. OntoViz is capable to visualize small ontologies in a very powerful manner. However, more advanced users criticize its performance and navigation issues under large ontologies. OntoGraf comes pre-installed with Protégé 5.0 and has a sophisticated and highly interactive graph layout. It is even powerful while working with large ontologies. Figure 10 shows a screenshot of OntoGraf used in Protégé.

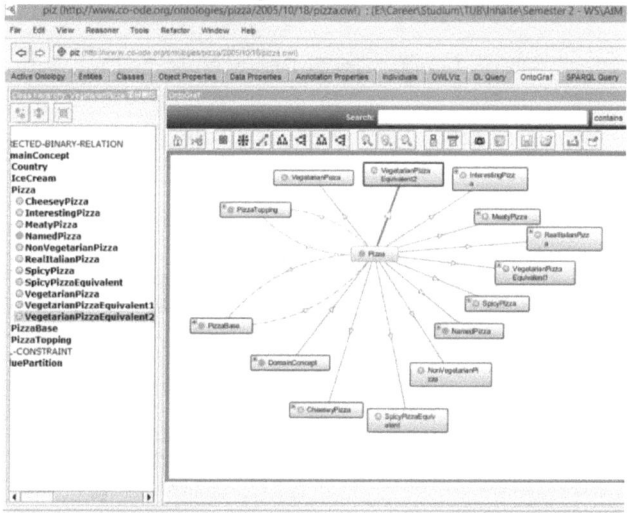

Figure 10 - Screenshot of OntoGraf in Protégé

4.4 Internals

To fully understand Protégé and its role as an ontology editor it is necessary to take an abstract view onto the architecture. Generally speaking, Protégé presents itself as a usual 3-layer information system containing a presentation layer, an application logic layer and a database layer.

In Figure 12 we present the architecture of Protégé-2000 as it has not essentially changed compared to its current version. Users are able to utilize user interfaces to access to Protégé's knowledge model API. Many different user interfaces are available, such as customizable slot and tab plug-ins, or even completely customized user interfaces. Furthermore, a variety of storage mechanisms are supported to store ontology data persistently. Flat files like default Protégé files, RDF, OWL, etc. can be stored as well as various different schemas in relational databases. It is important to mention that in all cases the developer is responsible to take care of the mappings between the core unit (application logic) and the persistent storage [15].

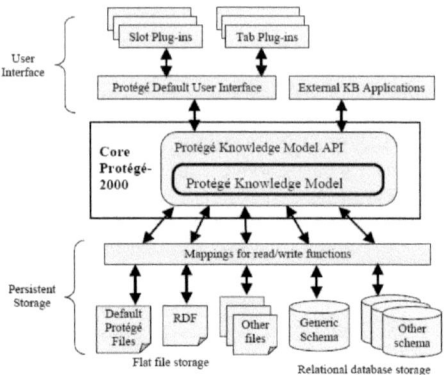

Figure 12 - Protégé-2000 architecture [15]

From this point of view we also want to take a look at the abstract architecture of WebProtégé (Figure 11). Besides WebProtégé was built to fully offer a product to collaboratively edit ontologies. Also, a collaborative desktop version of Protégé called Collaborative Protégé is available. This serves as another user interface, as WebProtégé is only web-based (available in web browsers and web applications). Based on those interfaces the user interacts with the system. Servlet engines are ready to serve the RPC and REST service calls coming from the web-based client side applications. As we already mentioned the web-based Protégé also fully supports OWL-formatted documents. Ultimately, all clients communicate with the collaboration framework via RMI. The collaboration framework offers all collaboration services like tracking changes and access control [48].

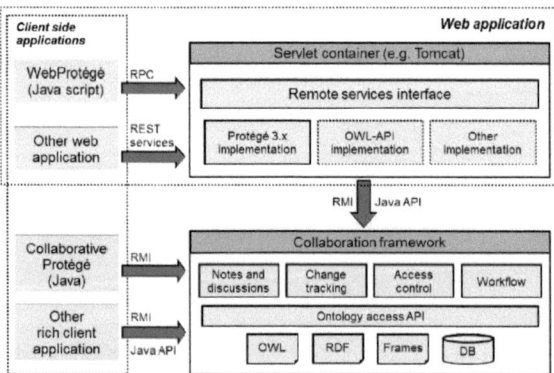

Figure 11 - WebProtégé architecture [48]

4.5 Building Ontologies

Generally building ontologies is an iterative approach that can be done by many different ways and always should concentrate on the concept - based on objects (nouns) and their relations (verbs). For Protégé there exists a suggested approach by Noy and McGuinnes [38]. Figure 13 shows the intended approach.

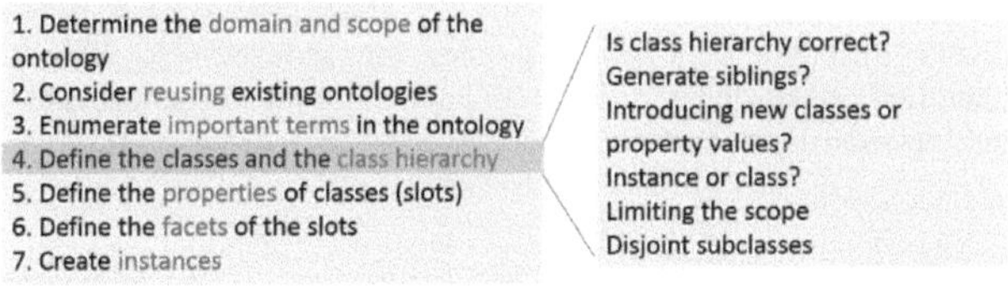

1. Determine the domain and scope of the ontology
2. Consider reusing existing ontologies
3. Enumerate important terms in the ontology
4. Define the classes and the class hierarchy
5. Define the properties of classes (slots)
6. Define the facets of the slots
7. Create instances

Is class hierarchy correct?
Generate siblings?
Introducing new classes or property values?
Instance or class?
Limiting the scope
Disjoint subclasses

Figure 13 - Suggested ontology creation approach by Noy and McGuinness [38]

4.6 Critical Appraisal

OWL is a very expressive and flexible data modelling language and superior compared to traditional data modelling techniques especially when it comes to searching. Protégé supports the modelling part in a very good manner and is extensible. Furthermore, Protégé is able to infer new knowledge automatically and to visualize ontologies. Also the trend of collaboration is addressed by Protégé.

Nonetheless, we have to criticize Protégé in some perspectives. The manual creation of ontologies is still very buggy. Reasoners have their limits, especially when it comes to the point of performance (rules and queries need to be optimized). Protégé is still a complex and confusing tool so that highly skilled engineers are required, especially for very big projects. The freedom Protégé offers referring to an editing and modelling approach can lead to failures. The fact is that the open-source perspective of Protégé can lead to an abundance of add-on tools and to confusion. WebProtégé has to prove itself.

5. Practical Applications

Although ontologies are widely used in theoretical research their importance in practical applications is even bigger. Because of their capabilities they can help to integrate data and create reusable knowledge. Furthermore, they support business and science to build flexible, efficient, consistent and reliable systems. Hereby, ontologies serve as a supporting tool when it comes to knowledge building or integration of heterogeneous information systems [44]. In the following we discover a selection of industry solutions where ontologies are widely used and support the business strategies and solutions. Furthermore, we name some large and widely-accepted ontologies of different industry and science fields. At last, we exemplary present the way Protégé is used in biomedical science, as the largest field of use.

5.1 Industry Solutions

Predominantly, ontologies are used in business solutions for searching and sharing large knowledge bases usually integrating many systems to a system that presents itself to the user as a standalone system [14],[49]. Recent projects, like the newly started venture SearchHaus [30], offer general purpose business solutions to integrate a variety of heterogeneous information systems in business environments (e.g. relational databases, data warehouses, ERP, triplestores). End-users have easy and intuitive access to all knowledge in the company with the input of simple keywords (adhoc-reporting with concrete questions). Another solution is called Ontology4™ [29] - a specialized tool for network service operators like telecommunication companies or internet service providers. The tool also searches data from a variety of information systems such as network data systems, CRM systems or even unstructured documents. The focus here lies on customer and network data to give user fast and reliable answers to their questions. Figure 14 shows the general approach behind Ontology4™. After different information sources are indexed and linked, errors are automatically identified and resolved. A dependency tree is built which serves as an ontology. Based on semantic relationships reasoning tools infer new knowledge.

Figure 14 - General ontology creation process in Ontology4™ (based on [29])

Other industry fields for searching and finding purposes which include ontologies are the oil and gas industry (e.g. Obtique [33]) and the logistics and supply chain management (e.g. OrGoLo [35]). Furthermore, ontologies are widely used for teaching purposes [11], or the development and operation of artificial intelligence (AI) and virtual assistants (e.g. IBM Watson [16], Apple Siri [7]).

5.2 Established Ontologies

There exist many ontologies that are already tested and embedded in many solutions. In this case it often makes sense to integrate those ontologies into projects where the development is still in progress rather than to develop own solutions. Especially, for the field of bio-informatics there is a large variety of existing ontologies like the Gene Ontology for genomics or the Disease Ontology for medicine. In the field of social ontologies the Friend of a Friend Ontology comes into consideration serving with the knowledge and terms about people and their behavior. Another interesting ontology would be the Geopolitical Ontology about politics. Also in the field of economics a variety of ontologies are available like the Financial Industry Business Ontology (FIBO) containing terms of the financial industry or the AGROVOC Ontology, containing terms of the agricultural industry. For the purpose of having access to a multilingual encyclopedia, the BabelNet Ontology would be one solution [22].

5.3 Biomedical Science and Protégé

As we mentioned earlier the ontology editor Protégé was initially used to serve in the field of biomedicine. In fact, Protégé is still used predominantly in a variety of biomedical science projects to represent biomedical knowledge bases (e.g. [6],[12],[34]) or using it for integration purposes of biomedical data sources [40]. Even further plugins are in development, e.g. for natural language processing in the biomedical field [47].

For instance [34] creates a framework (Figure 15) that is able to support adverse drug event (ADE) prevention in regards to a Clinical Decision Support System (CDSS). Their approach is the following: They systematically analyze and formalize the knowledge sources. The framework is based on Computer Interpretable Guidelines. The integration of diverse and dynamic knowledge sources follows. Protégé serves as a tool to represent the knowledge base. Figure 15 shows the framework architecture.

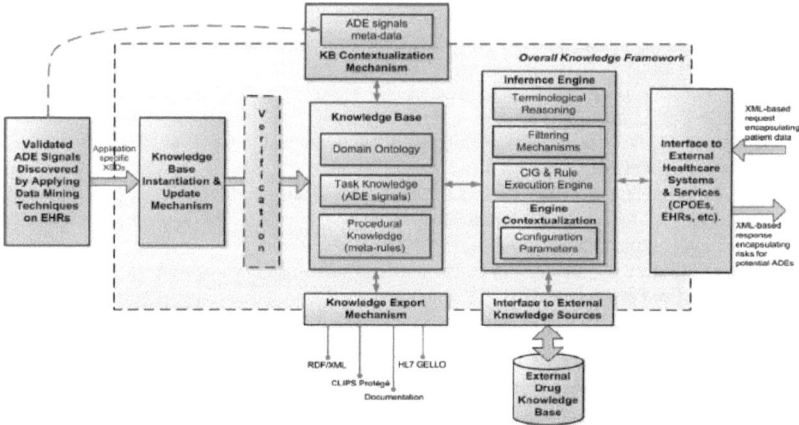

Figure 15 - Architecture of a knowledge framework for adverse drug event prevention [34]

6. Conclusion

In this paper we discovered the use of ontologies in practice. As ontologies are helpful in representing knowledge in a highly accessible model and are capable to verify and infer new knowledge, they help to overcome semantic heterogeneity. Ontology-based information integration can be addressed with a variety of semantic technologies, predominating OWL as it concludes machine-readable syntax with class description methods and semantic relationships. Prevalently, mappings support the integration of ontologies and other sources to build up an integrated data schema.

A huge variety of tools is available to support engineers and decision makers in knowledge engineering and integration tasks. For instance, the Protégé ontology editor is a well-established tool to model, validate and visualize ontologies even following the current trend of collaborative ontology engineering.

Many application fields of ontologies can be found in science and industry making use of ontologies main purposes which is the support of data integration by creating reusable, consistent, vivid and reliable knowledge in a flexible, efficient and extendible manner.

7. References

1. Agnar Aamodta, A., Nygårdb, M.: Different roles and mutual dependencies of data, information, and knowledge - an AI perspective on their integration. In: Data and Knowledge Engineering 16. (1995) 191-222
2. Akrivi, K., Elena, T., Constantin, H., Georgios, L., Costas, V.: A Comparative Study of Four Ontology Visualization Techniques in Protégé: Experiment Setup and Preliminary Results. (2006)
3. Alatrish, E.: Comparison Some of Ontology Editors. In Management Information Systems. Vol. 8 No. 2. (2013) 18-24
4. Baader, F.: The Description Logic Handbook: Theory, Implementation and Applications. Cambridge University Press. (2010)
5. Bodenreider, O., Stevens, R.: Bio-ontologies: current trends and future directions. In Briefings in Bioinformatics. Vol.7 No.3. (2006) 256-274
6. Bright, T.J., Furuya, E.Y., Kuperman, G.J., Cimino, J.J., Bakken, S.: Development and evaluation of an ontology for guiding appropriate antibiotic prescribing. In Journal of Biomedical Informatics 45. (2012) 120-128
7. Cheyer, A., Gruber, T.: Siri: A Virtual Personal Assistant - An Ontology-driven Application for the Masses. Siri. Presentation. (2010)
8. Choi, N., Song, I.-Y., Han, H.: A Survey on Ontology Mapping. In SIGMOD Record. Vol. 35. No. 3. (2006) 34-41
9. Data, Information, Knowledge, Wisdom Pyramid: http://www.allthingy.com/data-information-knowledge-wisdom/ Last retrieval: 20/01/2015
10. Dentler, K., Cornet, R., Teije, A.t., de Keizer, N.: Comparison of Reasoners for large Ontologies in the OWL 2 EL Profile. In Semantic Web 1. 1-5. IOS Press. (2011)
11. Devedzic, V.: Education and the Semantic Web. In International Journal of Artificial Intelligence in Education 14. (2004). 39-65
12. Dramé, K., Diallo, G., Delva, F., Dartigues, J.F., Mouillet, E., Salamon, R., Mougin, F.: Reuse of termino-ontological resources and text corpora for building a multilingual domain ontology: An application to Alzheimer's disease. In Journal of Biomedical Informatics 48. (2014) 171-182
13. Euzenat, J., Shvaiko, P.: Ontology Matching. Springer. (2013)
14. Franz., J., Traphöner, R.: Semantic Web for Knowledge Reuse in Business Processes. In Semantic Knowledge Management: Integrating Technologies. Springer. (2009) 215-230
15. Gennari, J.H., Musen, M.A., Fergerson, R.W., Grosso, W.E., Crubézy, M., Eriksson, H., Noy, N.F., Tu, S.W.: The evolution of Protégé: an environment for knowledge-based systems development. (2003)
16. Gliozzo, A., Biran, O., Patwardhan, S., McKeown, K.: Semantic Technologies in IBM Watson™. (2013)
17. Gruber, T.: Toward Principles for the Design of Ontologies Used for Knowledge Sharing. (1993)
18. Guo-jian and Rui-xue: A Review and Prospects on Collaborative Ontology Editing Tools, Journal of Integrative Agriculture, 2012, 11(5): 731-740.
19. Haarslev, V., Hidde, K., Möller, R., Wessel, M.: The RacerPro knowledge representation and reasoning system. (2012)
20. Horridge, M.: A Practical Guide to Building OWL Ontologies Using Protégé 4 and CO-ODE Tools Edition 1.3. University of Manchester. (2011)
21. Horrocks, I.: Ontologies and the Semantic Web. (2008)
22. http://en.wikipedia.org/wiki/Ontology_%28information_science%29 Last retrieval: 20/01/2015
23. http://protege.stanford.edu/ Last retrieval: 20/01/2015
24. http://protege.stanford.edu/products.php Last retrieval: 20/01/2015
25. http://protegewiki.stanford.edu/wiki/OntoGraf Last retrieval: 20/01/2015
26. http://protegewiki.stanford.edu/wiki/OntoViz Last retrieval: 20/01/2015
27. http://semanticweb.org/wiki/Tools Last retrieval: 20/01/2015
28. http://smiy.files.wordpress.com/2011/01/sw_layercake.png, Last retrieval: 20/01/2015

29. http://www.ontology.com/ Last retrieval: 20/01/2015
30. http://www.searchhaus.net/en/ Last retrieval: 20/01/2015
31. Kashyap, V., Bussler, C., Moran, M.: The Semantic Web. Springer. (2008)
32. Katifori, A., Halatsis, C., Lepouras, G., Vassilakis, C., Giannopoulou, E.: Ontology visualization methods—A survey. In ACM Comput. Surv. 39. 4. Article 10. (2007)
33. Kharlamov, E., Jiménez-Ruiz, E., Zheleznyakov, D., Bilidas, D., Giese, M., Haase, P., Horrocks, I., Kllapi, H., Koubarakis, M., Özcep, Ö., Rodriguez-Muro, M., Rosati, R., Schmidt, M., Schlatte, R., Soylu, A., Whaaler, A.: Optique: Towards OBDA Systems for Industry. In The Semantic Web: ESWC 2013 Satellite Events. (2013) 125-140
34. Koutkias, V., Kilintzis, V., Stalidis, G., Lazou, K., Niés, J., Durand-Texte, L. ,McNair, P., Beuscart, R., Maglaveras, N.: Knowledge engineering for adverse drug event prevention: On the design and development of a uniform, contextualized and sustainable knowledge-based framework. In Journal of Biomedical Informatics 45. (2012) 495-506
35. Kowalski, M., Quink, N.: OrGoLo-Projektbericht Nr.16: Erstellung einer Ontologie zum Themenkomplex Verpackungen in der Logistik mithilfe des Ontologie-Editors Protégé. Effizienzcluster Ruhr-Essen. (2013)
36. Leser, U., Naumann, F.: Information Integration. (2007)
37. McGuinness D.L., van Harmelen F.: OWL Web Ontology Language Overview. W3C Recommendation. (2004)
38. Noy, N.F., McGuinness, D.L.: Ontology Development 101: A Guide to Creating Your First Ontology. (2001)
39. Olivé, A.: Conceptual Modeling of Information Systems. Springer. (2007)
40. Post, A.R., Kurc, T., Cholleti, S., Gao, J., Lin, X., Bornstein, W., Cantrell, D., Levine, D., Hohmann, S., Saltz, J.H.: The Analytic Information Warehouse (AIW): A platform for analytics using electronic health record data. In Journal of Biomedical Informatics 46. (2013) 410-424
41. Prud'hommeaux, E., Seaborne A.: SPARQL Query Language for RDF. W3C Recommendation. (2008)
42. Racer Systems GmbH & Co. KG: RacerPro Reference Manual, Version 1.9. (2010)
43. Rebstock, M., Janina, F., Paulheim, H., Naujok, K.-D., Huemer, C., Röder, P., Tafreschi, O.: Ontologies-Based Business Integration. Springer. (2008)
44. Staab, S: Handbook on ontologies. Springer. (2004)
45. Stanley, R., McManus, B., Ng, R., Gombocz, E., Eshleman, J., Rockey, C.: Case Study: Applied Semantic Knowledgebase for Detection of Patients at Risk of Organ Failure through Immune Rejection, Stanley et al. IO Informatics, Inc., Berkeley, CA, USA, 2011
46. Rajendran, A., Cruz, I.F.: Semantic Data Integration in Hierarchical Domains. In IEEE Intelligent System. 18 (2). (2003) 66-73
47. Tao, C., Song, D., Sharma, D., Chute, C.G.: Semantator: Semantic annotator for converting biomedical text to linked data. In Journal of Biomedical Informatics 46. (2013) 882-893
48. Tudorache, T., Nyulas, C., Noy, N.F., Musen, M.A.: WebProtégé: A Collaborative Ontology Editor and Knowledge Acquisition Tool for the Web. In Semantic Web. IOS Press. 1-0. (2011) 1-11
49. Tran, D.T., Herzig, D.M., Ladwig, G.: SemSearchPro – Using semantics throughout the search process. (2011)
50. Wache H., Vögele, T., Vissar, U., Stuckenschmidt, H., Schuster, G., Neumann, H., Hübner, S.: Ontology-Based Integration of Information - A Survey of Existing Approaches. In Proceedings of IJCAI-01 Workshop: Ontologies and Information Sharing. (2001) 108-117
51. Wächter, T., Fabian, G., Schroeder, M.: DOG4DAG: semi-automated ontology generation in OBO-Edit and Protégé. In Proceedings of the 4th International Workshop on Semantic Web Applications and Tools for the Life Sciences (SWAT4LS '11). (2011)
52. Wang, H., Noy, N., Rector., A., Musen, M., Redmond., T., Rubin, D., Tu, S., Tudorache, T., Drummond, N., Horridge, M., Seidenberg, J.: Frames and OWL side by side. 9th Intl. Protege Conference, Stanford, California. (2006)